BE
HOLDING

PITT POETRY SERIES ED OCHESTER, EDITOR

ROSS
GAY

BE
HOLDING

A POEM

UNIVERSITY OF PITTSBURGH PRESS

Published by the University of Pittsburgh Press, Pittsburgh, Pa., 15260

Manufactured in the United States of America

Printed on acid-free paper

10 9 8 7 6 5 4 3 2 1

ISBN 13: 978-0-8229-6623-4

ISBN 10: 0-8229-6623-9

COVER ART: "This Negro woman lives with her husband and two grand-children in an old converted schoolhouse. All the rest of her children have left the county. Heard County, Georgia" by Jack Delano. Library of Congress Prints and Photographs Division Washington, D.C. 20540 USA

BOOK AND COVER DESIGN: Joel W. Coggins

Bound in gratitude

This poem does not exist without the work and ideas and words of many, many writers and thinkers, among them Amiri Baraka, Garnette Cadogan, Toi Derricotte, Aracelis Girmay, Saidiya Hartman, Allen Iverson, Fred Moten, Kevin Quashie, Patrick Rosal, Christina Sharpe, and Susan Sontag. By which I mean the work and thinking and care and words are indebted to them, and are sometimes actually theirs.

About Dr. J

It has occurred to me, with much sorrow (though I'm getting over it), that not everyone knows who Dr. J (Julius Erving) is. I have learned this over the years, as I was trying to write this poem and would occasionally be talking to, shall we say, *millenials*, about what I was working on.

"Oh," I'd say vaguely, "I'm working on a poem about Dr. J." In these encounters I realized that many of these otherwise decent people had never heard of The Doctor (though LeBron James, et a few al., they had all mostly at least heard of).

This strikes me as a generational ignorance, not a moral one, and for that reason I begrudge these people (or you, if you are one of them) not at all, for I have never read *Harry Potter*, etc., etc., etc., etc., and feel at least in the realm of being a decent person.

Anyhow, for this poem to be its most . . . you know, whatever a poem might be to you, it might behoove you to do a teeny bit of research on Dr. J. You could just look on any of the video algorithm machines, or watch the *The Doctor*, a Dr. J documentary narrated by Chuck D.

Or, better yet, you could just ask an elder. Which, incidentally, in addition to being someone who knows who Dr. J is, is a kind of tree or shrub from whose ripe black berries you can make a potent antiviral medicine, useful prophylactically and after infection.

BE
HOLDING

. . . to be held. To behold

CHRISTINA SHARPE,
IN THE WAKE: ON BLACKNESS AND BEING

BE HOLDING

APRIL 4, 2015—TODAY

You might have noticed there's nowhere to go,
the wind cutting little eddies

at your collarbones
and behind your ear,

as Dr. J drives from the foul line extended
to the baseline, defended valiantly

by Mark Landsberger, who, in this poem,
despite the doofy urge to make him so,

is not allegorical,
but is rather simply a hardworking journeyman

ball player with decent athleticism and size
and a floppy mop of dusty blond hair

got caught up in the gust,
sliding his size 16s quick

so that Doc, after catching the ball at the elbow
and taking one hard dribble toward the baseline

where the dunk would usually commence,
could not access the paint,

or the lane, or *the key*, which is what
we call the area nearest the goal,

which, in this case,
is an iron hole drawn in space,

and therefore implies a window
though the key makes it also a door

that Landsberger, it seemed,
was trying to keep shut,

and so Doc leapt,
he *left his feet,*

which means more or less jumping with the ball
with nowhere to go, and which

we're warned against by coaches
from day one

for the ensuing requisite stupid pass
or more simply though no less stupid

travel, also called *walking,*
which the leaping often leads to,

keep your feet!
again and again,

which makes the leaping—leaving your feet—
sound sacrificial,

the way in certain places, certain
countries, or countries inside of countries,

you must leave by foot with nowhere to go,
which there is,

and Doc, you should note, after the one dribble
clasps the ball with only his right hand

without once at all in any shape or form
using the left, which, *among other things*,

friends, differentiates this from all
the descendant moves—

Kevin Durant, Dwyane Wade,
Steph and Giannis and Harden and Kawhi,

yes, Bron Bron too,
I shall not be moved—

and using only one hand,
which is amazing but not yet miraculous,

more a physical and therefore genetic fact
(thanks Ma & Pa Erving),

Doc's hand becomes an octopus
gripping the ball nothing like prey,

and with that ball snugged in his mitt
Doc maybe kinda sorta thought something like

I am going to put this schmuck
(the schmuck in this case being Landsberger,

though do not, please, revert to a simplistic
allegorization of the journeyman,

which word I repeat advisedly)
on a poster,

though schmuck is a word I'd be
surprised to hear Doc say,

and the word *posterize,*
(common usage: *posterize his ass)*

you might be thinking,
is a bit of an anachronism in this poem,

in this move, which ostensibly occurred
in the 1980 NBA Finals,

though we all know that nothing happens
only when it happens,

we all know nothing happens
only when it happens,

emerging more in the epoch
(which in the NBA lasts 3-5 years)

following Doc's retirement—
Nique and Jordan,

Hakeem the Dream and Clyde the Glide,
Barkley, The Glove,

and yo, remember Shawn Kemp?—
though Doc probably thought it anyway,

visionary that he was, *when will they verb*
what I keep doing

to these schmucks,
especially Bill fucking Walton,

driving from the foul line extended
toward the baseline

as the unsuspecting Landsberger
who did a fine job

of shuffling his size 16s and not holding,
keeping Erving from the key,

and who must for a scant
and fleeting moment

have felt a degree of pride
when Doc, after the hard dribble right,

left his feet with nowhere to go,
Billy Cunningham on the sideline,

his hands on his hips,
his sport coat thrown open,

a few strands of hair stuck
to his moist pink brow

and almost smiling
as Doc began sailing

out of bounds, over the baseline,
and Landsberger, a solid leaper, skied

and foreclosed the possibility of Doc
sneaking a shot in

this side of the basket
(by which I mean dunking probably quite hard)

by putting his hand against the backboard
—a big door swinging shut—

at which fine and commendable defensive effort
Erving simply decided in the air

to knock on other doors
by soaring more

—have you ever decided *anything*
in the air?—

turtling his head into his chest
so as not to bash it

against the backboard,
flying like that, in fact, now

behind the basket and backboard
where Kareem, a good help defender

—umm, wait a sec, that's wrong—
Kareem, one of the best defenders *of all time*,

5 time NBA All-Defensive first team,
6 time NBA All-Defensive second team,

6 MVPs (sorry MJ),
not to mention

(which means it requires mentioning),
Kareem was one of those Negroes

they changed the rules for,
banning the dunk for years from the NCAA,

which is to say
banning emphatic and exquisite flight,

which maybe explains
the wise and sort of tired eyes of

Kareem, *one of the best basketball players
of all time,*

who had slid to also cut off the baseline,
which he accomplished,

but found himself now looking into the sky
directly out of bounds,

which his own suddenly unfamiliar
body must have been telling him

was so weird,
this is so weird,

looking and looking like this,
his hands extended timidly,

a silver maple's branches
creaking and swaying

in a hurricane,
for Doc was amongst the trees

as we call the big men
like Kareem, *the trees,*

who reside mostly in the lane,
or in the key,

growing there, rooting,
the thousands of fans now

holding their breath, looking
into the sky, some of their hands

reaching out instinctively toward their neighbors
beside them, or their palms

instinctively laying on the shoulders
before them, or forearms shoved

gently into a wrist or hip beside them,
a few arms of strangers suddenly locked

as if going for a stroll,
the whole of the Spectrum

become a kind of dew-glistened web
shivering its gems in the gales

as Erving went higher
and now began

to extend his right hand in a precise arc
beginning precisely above his head,

painting a broad and precise circle
not unlike Leonardo's *Vitruvian Man*

in his hula hoop
of perfect proportions

(if that little naked man wasn't little
or naked and was palming a basketball

and was flying
through the trees)

and I find myself again and again with my arm
making the perfectly impossible circle

again and again
as I watch this clip on YouTube

frame by frame clumsily
on a computer with gummy keys

and a Post-it note
covering the eyehole scrawled

DISCIPLINE
on April 5, 2015,

at 1:48 a.m., again
and again, thinking

what am I looking at,
what am I seeing,

back to the first long step toward the baseline,
the slight contact with Landsberger,

the leap, again,
long step, contact,

leap, again, long step,
contact, leap,

again, long step, contact, leap,
and I notice this time

in the background,
which is, granted, hazy,

this being old footage and my eyes a bit rheumy
for the now nearly two hours studying this clip,

I notice, at about the foul line, Silk,
aka Jamaal Wilkes,

who, for the record, Coach Wooden,
on the record, said was his best player ever at UCLA,

not Kareem and
oh fuck forever Bill Walton,

and it's worthwhile to spend at least a moment
with the name Silk,

among the finest basketball nicknames,
implying an ease and fluidity of movement,

implying a difficult thing,
a painful thing,

made to look easy,
a fiber prized for its softness,

its smoothness on the skin,
gathered from captive worms

fed mulberry leaves,
my court name was Beast

for what it's worth,
and after a summer league game

on the court at 10th and Lombard
where those in the know

would slide through a gap
in the grimace of the wrought iron gate

to get in, a court that would be in time
shut down in the most heinous

of ways—removing the rims—
the backboards lonely as gravestones—

because of complaints to the city
from the condo owners

across the street
who did not want to hear god forbid

all that Negro gathering
and celebration and care and delight

every goddamn weekend morning
all that

frolic and tumult,
all that *flight*,

(*why can't they just go
someplace else?*)

a slightly older opponent
told me, holding

my hand and shoulder
and pulling me close

—he was holding me—
beneath the stately oaks

overhanging the court,
looking kindly down on us

and time to time
blocking a high arcing shot

and wishing a leaf or two upon
the ex-ballers on the sidelines

reading the *Philadelphia Inquirer*,
sipping coffee, debating and laughing

or acting stupid like refs making calls
oh yeah he walked his ass off,

the oaks dappling the oldheads and their discourse
(the best line of verse I will ever write),

his shirt soaked through,
staring at me to be sure

I was listening, which I was, then as now,
you aint no beast, you aint

no beast, you're a man,
you hear me,

I notice Silk's right leg and hip twitch
before relaxing with what might have been the body's *aw shit*

though if you look closely,
again and again,

in a certain kind of way,
again and again,

you'll see also what might be a kind of light
descending upon Silk's high cheekbones

and forehead, again and again,
unfurling almost across his face

as he cranes his neck toward the soaring
until you'd almost swear, tonight,

at 2:26 a.m., he was looking into
a tree strewn with people,

the human-shaped shadows twisting
across his body, the legs swaying into his torso,

a gray hand birding across his face,
resting for a second at his ear,

the pinky become a beak from which
wheezed a tiny song, you'd swear,

watching this sliver of the clip
again and again,

the shadow of one man's head seeming to lay itself
on Silk's chest, for which, in the clip,

you'll see Silk make of his arm
a cradle, lowering his head

as though to say *I'm sorry,*
I'm so sorry,

with which the tree makes a kind of choir,
moaning, *I'm so sorry,*

twisting its roots in the molder
with what they've been made to do,

wait—wait—
what am I looking at—

what am I
practicing—

it's not that, no no,
it's not that,

it's late, my eyes are playing tricks,
for this tree is like the biggest Uncle

at the biggest family reunion
holding in its flung open arms

9 guys both raucous and rapt
hollering and smacking hands and holding each other

cooing like lovebirds
for the flight they're amidst

in one of the house's best seats
at Rucker Park in Harlem

where the young as-yet-un-pseudonymous
Julius Erving,

just a college kid from UMass,
has begun his extended course of study

on gravity and grace,
which has so enthralled the throngs

some kids scale the court's chain link fence
looking like belly-bared scarabs with bell-bottoms

and Chuck Taylors, and some peer
from the bridge beyond, the traffic itself

slowed, and a couple hundred lounge
precariously on ledges outside

school windows, backpacks tucked
in their laps or under their butts,

one boy laying on his side
with a small stack of schoolbooks wedged

beneath his close-shorn head,
the algebraic equations tumbling

into his ear as he looks drowsily down on the court
and beyond from the ledge, his left arm dangling

and casting slow eddies into the air,
and do you know while composing this

I almost dreamed some doom
upon that child

dozing beautifully in my poem
dreaming now above the flying—

what am I
looking at

what am I
practicing

—he sprawled there in the sun
easy as a lizard,

while the gangly fella below
with knee-high socks

and well-shaped fro
and the wispy beginnings of a goatee

and a mouth perched somewhere between
you better not and *isn't this lovely*

with little fanfare though no small delight
again and again flies to the rim

this time on the 6'9" post player
after having threaded and flummoxed the two guards at the foul line

and cranking the ball with one hand back
far enough that, if he so chose,

he could have dropped it easily
into the back pocket

of his rather short shorts,
the big man himself a good player

in the NBA, watching from below
holding his breath to see

what I'm telling you
about Erving's soaring,

which is less its astronauticality,
and more the cast of the young

Erving's eyes, which are looking, somehow,
far past the metal backboards

or the rim he would, imminently,
rock the rust from, looking far

past the chain link
wrapping the courts and past the high-rise

apartments and past the elevated tracks
of the Metro-North he rode to get here,

and past the Hudson's muddy haul
and the gulls swirling above

in the gusts, and looking
far past that, even, the big man sees,

and seeing Doc seeing like that the big man thinks
what is Julius looking at,

before feeling, strangely,
entering into his nose

and mouth, the damp salty air
of a sea coast which flashes him to Coney Island,

where the night before he and his boys
gobbled fries at Nathan's before strolling

the boardwalk and three times fell hard in love,
mostly with themselves,

hugging and shoving blent unbeknownst
into the ratty beach plum's fragrance

which, the big man can tell, this breeze isn't quite,
some as yet indiscernible difference

as the coastal air's brine
braids with his own salt and grime,

during which he even looks at his own large hands,
a gesture of doubt and faith both,

sinking his face into them
and inhaling and hearing

again and again
the soft exhalation of water

scurrying onto a beach
and tumbling back into the sea,

the impossibly fine chatter
of shell fragments rattling in the furl,

the sizzle of tiny crabs skittering
across the slickened sand, and the wet kiss

of seaweed unwrapping on a shore,
and a softer sound still

of water slithering through the reeds of a saltmarsh,
all of which, yes, is truly strange, I think,

my Chuck Taylors sinking just so
into the sand with wisps of beach grass

shivering against my shins, *this is so strange,*
as a human sound now comes from the water,

or more, perhaps, a net of human voices
harmonizing with the water, threading with the lash

of waves withdrawing into the collective hush
of Rucker Park, you can see,

in the photos, from the schoolkids' faraway gaze,
and the far cast of the men embraced by the tree,

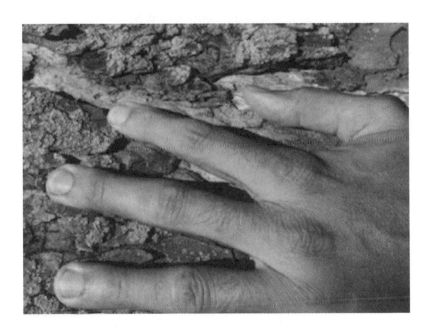

the soft grooves and crevices of their hands
laid against the soft grooves and crevices of the tree

their human hands all gently grasping a limb
as if to say *look, look,*

until they become one slow-breathing animal
with 18 legs and arms and 10 hearts

looking into the near distance
where a human song was lapping from the waves,

lifting from beyond an anchored and just-listing
ship, newly ballast free,

barnacled and slapped at by breaking wakes,
its tar-blacked boards

whining and gasping even at rest,
and waking from the song

beyond the ship
as though from the ship

a woman looked somehow as though
she was ascending a staircase,

first timidly, and then trusting the thrust
of her knees and hips and two good feet,

taking them by twos, bounding,
and soon behind came someone else,

bounding and soaring,
and someone else,

and someone else, until the ship itself
seemed to drag its anchor, twisting to see,

and the live oaks too,
turning beneath their shawls of moss,

and the acres and acres of pines
and the people

felling them and
hewing them

into planks for ships
like the ones those now in the sky came on

lean into each other and look,
and look, until is gathered

a small village above the low clouds
hovering now as much as soaring,

their arms outstretched as if treading water,
their hands and feet making small circles,

their chains dangling and slicing rusty wakes
into the air until one by one

they shake loose and tumble from their ankles and wrists
erasing through the sky and into the sea

like names disappearing from a ledger,
hovering there like a school

looking down at us,
watching,

as Doc continues his flight
over the baseline,

his arm extended in the midst of its cyclone,
for a glimpse cantilevered like a Frank Lloyd Wright

building beneath which pours a sometimes tempestuous
stream, and watching the move

again and again like this
at 2:59 a.m. I notice now

when Doc is suspended here
in his flight Kareem's hands no longer look

like the flimsy limbs of silver maples
but like a person preparing

to catch a falling body,
which maybe explains the worry stitching itself

across Kareem's face and the nervous
bend of his legs, maybe explains

the way he seems to contract his whole torso,
his heart's carriage, by holding his breath,

and the 18,168 spectators in this clip
whom I have seen hundreds of times tonight

explode with delight
I notice now their outreached hands

take the same instinctive posture of primates
falling through air, which is thought to have emerged

that we might grab a branch on our plummet
with our downturned palms,

and not die,
which might be an act of bodily sympathy

we do unwittingly when witnessing
the unwitnessable, the way

we do so often these days,
today, witness the unwitnessable,

my own palms twisted again and again
toward the earth,

witnessing the unwitnessable,
which is not unlike their motion

treading water
in a college gallery

for mostly wealthy white children
exhibiting its special collection of photography,

a Lincoln portrait and display of weird
Warhol photos, a young Sly Stallone among them,

when I rounded the partition, and between the famous
war photo of the Viet Cong colonel

in the midst of his being publicly executed,
wincing and his hair mussed as though a small bird

had just flown from his ear, and the famous
war photo of the naked child fleeing

the wreckage of her own napalmed skin,
was the famous photo

of two black people falling
from a collapsed fire escape,

the adult near the bottom of the photo tumbled
into a dive, her left forearm and hand

elegantly drawn into what could be a wave
but is not, obscuring her face,

though behind the tiny gully at her wrist
is her eyebrow and the slight shadow

cast by the small cave of her eye socket
and what it was seeing,

and falling also in the looking
a common houseplant

that must have sat on the fire escape
and that she must have watered time to time,

or poured in her spent coffee grounds
like her aunt showed her,

and sang with the plant, as we do, quietly,
feathering her fingers through the fronds

loving you-ooh is easy
'cause you're beautifu-u-ul

before gently plucking with her thumb and forefinger
some withered petals papery and gold

and blowing them like wishes
over the rail and watching them

flicker in and out of the light
to the lot below,

after which she might scoop up
the child and be

holding her as the moon
drifts into the horizon

of the building across the way,
which some nights

was the sail
of a ship,

and others a giant bird's
luminous plume

dancing on the far side
of the earth,

the baby
dozing in the hold

of the woman's
rocking arms,

the plant falling still mostly
upright beneath and just behind her,

her feet bare,
her arms outstretched

like one ready
to catch a child,

and above her falling
a child

with arms in the midst of their flail
splayed exactly unlike a bird

with her wings
unleashed against the wind,

her left leg drawn up nearly parallel
to her left arm,

the baby's little body
a frozen glyph,

the left foot's tiny saddle shoe
perfectly tied

by the hands of the woman
falling beneath her,

her tummy made bare
by the uprush of air

beneath her shirt,
her face tense

atop her shoulders drawn up slightly,
the tiny fingers on her tiny hands

spread wide and grasping,
she is holding her breath,

she is holding her breath,
I am holding my breath

with this looking
and looking

as she looks almost directly into the camera
which is to say

she sees herself being seen
shot captured

fixed
falling to her death

and held like that
unlovingly by the camera

behind which
was a man

in a building across the way
in a window

he found open to the horror
who would win a Pulitzer Prize for spot photography

for shooting the woman
and the little girl

capturing her
staring at us

staring at her death
whom I have not yet named

—you have seen, I hope—
for in the photograph neither are they named,

given as the photograph's two titles
are *Marlborough Street Fire*

and *Fire Escape Collapse,*
and imply no violence or horror upon these two people,

but rather upon the street, upon the fire escape which, true,
falls apart like a ship's deck dismantling in a storm,

and though they have memories,
though they too might moan

in sorrow if we listen closely,
they are not the people falling in the photo,

which the unnaming dreams, falling,
the natural state of these two people,

falling the natural state
of these people,

dying the natural
state of those people,

and it is while thinking upon this photo
which, nestled between the two iconic

war photographs in this gallery,
tended gently by a friendly white woman,

visited by classes of mostly but not all white children
checking their phones,

mostly not noticing
their noticing

and always have been,
mostly not noticing

we're noticing
and always have been,

the black people falling forever
framed on the pristine white wall

becomes itself
a war photograph,

though it is upon researching the photograph
I found not only the names of the falling,

Diana Bryant and Tiare Jones,
but also an article

from a regional newspaper in Virginia
celebrating some of the other Pulitzer winners,

among whom were Saul Bellow
for his novel *Humboldt's Gift*,

and R. W. B. Lewis for a biography of Edith Wharton,
and along with the article was a photo

of little Tiare Jones, survived,
my god thank god,

looking at the photo
of herself falling

slightly above her godmother,
pointing to herself in the image,

that's me falling
forever,

and pointing to her godmother,
whom she most likely had a sweet name for,

the way my nieces call my mother Munga
and me Uncle Rossy,

and whose fallen body broke her own fall,
and died in the breaking,

what I mean,
what I am saying—

But let's breathe first.
We're always holding our breath.

Let's stop and breathe,
you and me.

—is that someone took a picture
of the child Tiare Jones

looking at herself
falling forever

witnessing
the unwitnessable

what I mean
what I am saying

someone *decided* to take
a picture of a little black girl

decided to shoot
a little black girl

pointing and smiling at a photograph of herself
forever falling to her death

—Come on now. Breathe.
Let's try to keep breathing—

and no one took the photographer,
as he was on one knee adjusting tenderly

his lens with the tenderest parts
of his thumb and first two fingers,

bringing the child into sharp focus for capture,
and squinting and chirping directions,

can you smile for me honey,
can you point to yourself in the picture sweetie,

can you point to your dead
godmother and yourself forever falling

honey, putting their hands over the lens
and guiding it toward the photographer's hip,

before pinning him to the wall by his collar
or arm and whispering deep

so no one else could hear
(birdsong sack of axes

birdsong sickle
beckon the wrist)

singing forever in his ear
take that photograph

and I will cut the eyes from your head
for he was simply

doing his job,
adding his small work,

his touch,
to the museum

of black pain,
thrown overboard

for the insurance,
and of course now that I'm breathing

I wonder if, no,
I wonder *how,*

I, too, am a docent
in the museum of black pain,

if I might make a good salary,
paid vacations, benefits,

if I might be building a home
of our pain,

throwing myself overboard
for the insurance

what's my study
what's my practice

what are we
trading in

what are we
looking at

my arms now
cutting circles in the air,

imitating again Doc's arms whirling,
and I notice anew at 3:11 the precision and elegance

with which Doc knows when and for how long
to pull his head toward his heart

so as not to smash it into the glass backboard
which would, at this speed and angle,

hurt him bad or kill him,
the goal made missile by Doc's flight

sailing just above his right ear,
the daily evasion of which is,

as you know,
a version of genius,

like Donny Hathaway says of Stevie Wonder
before covering "Superwoman"

on *These Songs for You, Live!*
the Fender Rhodes like water

rocking in wakes above your body,
though he says it like this,

From the black pool of genius
we'd like to give you our rendition of

which, though I think
he was speaking nautically,

like a swimming pool,
or a tidepool or gene pool,

tonight I hear as the black *pull* of genius,
as in the black *tether* of genius,

the black rope the black
gravity the black

umbilicus of genius,
before Donny

walks into Wonder's song
and makes of it something,

somehow, like walking softly
from the grasping hands of the sea,

Oh Donny,
come back

as a flower,
Doc's head drooping

(iris tulip
violet lilac)

as though he were listening to some music
no one else had yet heard

coming from his body,
which you would likely miss

if you didn't watch the clip
as many times as we have tonight,

during which it looks like
Landsberger maybe fouled Doc

by putting his big armpit nearly into Doc's ear,
but truth is Doc cleared out gorgeously

with his left forearm
to make for himself space

through which to soar
(Shout out to little Ronnie Free

who I coached at Piscataway High School,
and when I went to block his shot,

like I swatted all the other pipsqueaks
learning slowly to attack the rim from the corner

—pump fake, two
dribbles, fly to the rim—

cleared out prophetically
with his elbow and laid

two of my bottom teeth down,
the ones going kind of gray,

and numb, his teammates all
clutching each other *oooooohhhhh!*,

he turned me into a window)
as he kept running into the sky

as though climbing a great staircase
made of air with joy,

which was not though should have been the name
of the dance move my friend Timmy

perfected the summer of 1989,
as though climbing a great staircase

made of air with joy
on the yellow curb where we put our little boombox

and played that summer mostly Heavy D and Special Ed
and Kwame and New Edition and Troop,

the trillion rubythroats trilling
their fleet wings inside our torsos

blazed with impatiens and torch flower
and bee balm though it was wolves

were said were in our bodies,
wilding and animal,

the wolves
we heard it

even if we didn't know
we heard it,

we saw it
even if we didn't know

we saw it,
and yes, we reeked of Drakkar

and the magic stank musk
of boys wildly

alive, and Timmy would engine
his arms and shoulders

at first as though whirling a quick cabbage patch,
before sinking into a squat

from which he'd spin back upright while
typhooning centrifugally, his head dipping to his chest

as though evading something
we knew but couldn't see,

little astilbe little trillium
little delphinium drowsing in the rain

to *Spread My Wings*
(*and fly away*

to the place that I long for)
fast enough that in my memory the cinders

spinning from the asphalt glowed
and a small fire would ignite

and Timmy became a twisting piston,
falling then flying,

falling then flying,
which too he'd help me to do,

holding my shoulders
and helping me lower myself slowly,

again and again, carrying me down
and guiding me up,

forearms beneath my armpits from behind,
our sweaty cheeks touching

as though ascending a great staircase
made of air with joy,

like this he'd be
holding me,

struggling, for I was
a corpulent pubescer,

before we'd both almost topple,
we'd both almost fall,

laughing hard,
when my legs would finally give mostly out,

and I'd bounce up
to Roger Rabbit or kick-step,

and one night
we went to Timmy's apartment to get some lemonade

and look at his new drawings
of the character he'd been perfecting the past year or two,

KOR, aka The King of Rock
(*there is none higher!*),

his folks tucked away in the den watching TV,
and after he put the sketchbook in my hand

of the iron creature
with slits in the metal for eyes

and stegosaurus spikes staggered
the length of his steel suit's back,

and while I was holding his imagination in my hands,
Timmy reached into the cupboard beneath the sink

and dipped his thumb and forefinger into a small box
with a picture of a cartoon rat with x's for eyes,

and slipping the pinch of poison
into his mouth, without wince,

while looking at me, said,
to get stronger,

then offered the dead rat to me,
reaching toward me

as I fell away,
holding my breath,

my arms cutting wakes
into the air around us,

and what I haven't yet said is when watching
the slow motion YouTube video,

which kindly shows the move in something like real time
before slowing it way down,

so that you and I can study it like this
and see what maybe is actually happening,

there is a flash at :23,
presumably from a camera

anticipating one of Doc's miracles,
though not this one,

and in the slow motion video
the flash occurs precisely at the moment

that Landsberger fulfills his obligation
detouring Erving from the key

and Kareem slides down with his long arm preparing
to toss Doc's shot somewhere toward oblivion,

and you notice now before the flash
Doc was probably just intending

to dunk simply though emphatically
on his own side of the hoop,

but was compelled to soar like this,
we've gone over this,

and in the slow motion video
that I am now tabbing forward incrementally,

studying forever each minute nuance
of this black person in flight,

I notice, I see, the entire screen
is blinded by that camera's flash,

with only the faintest ghosts apparent,
the red stripes of Doc's socks,

his jersey's 6, the red backboard square,
but the rest of the court,

and the players on it,
invisible, pixelated,

as though their real bodies
have disappeared into the screen,

as though their real lives have disappeared
into the screen,

and the disappearing
has become their lives,

and what I cannot help but think
tonight, at 3:33 a.m., a bit dazed, admittedly,

from watching Erving's move,
again, and again,

is that this
is like looking

at the surface of the water
from below,

is like looking into the sky
through the water's slow turning above

where you can squint and see bodies
looking down at you,

their slow light snapped
by one of the handful of photographers

kneeling in prayer at the baseline
(this, remember, before the ESPN era,

which, yes, there was a before to),
and inside of that flash where

Doc nearly disappears,
the airborne body become

so quick the absence
the light makes,

I so badly want the flash
I want the light

like a virus
blinding the screen

and the flight in it
to be a window,

or a door,
a door,

which right now I will point you to,
a real door in a real photograph

I found looking through the WPA agriculture photos
at the Library of Congress

for my great-grandfather
as a young man, a sharecropper in Osceola, Arkansas,

with hands like a hummingbird's,
who could fill his sacks

kind of quick plus a bit more
to sell on the side, which,

in the parlance of the day—
the same parlance as ours, incidentally,

in which you can own stolen land,
in which you can become very wealthy

owning stolen land, which all owned land is,
stolen goods, hot, hot goods,

the hot earth,
which earth has been bequeathed

as property, as heritable wealth,
though the meek shall first

inherit the heat,
but the land,

the cotton, the unshared crop,
let's hereon call it what it is,

loot, plain and simple,
which, too,

my great-grandfather's body was,
loot, and his life, *loot*,

his life was theirs,
like the crop,

like the land,
they could be,

they have been,
thrown overboard

for the insurance
(breathe; let's breathe)—

was *theft*,
which is to say,

it was his life
he was stealing,

steal away,
steel a way,

and caught
my great-grandfather was

made to quickly theorize
both flight and disappearance

by carving with a sickle
a crude window

into a man who mistook him for a door
he could open and close at will,

yes we come from poets,
steel a way,

and he stepped through
that window

by sitting on the sill
and lifting first his one leg

into his chest,
and like that looked for a moment

as though he was resting,
how I wish

he could rest,
as though he was just a young man

enjoying the day,
looking upon the family of oaks

near the road, their limbs
always like arms to him,

the shadows the leaves cast
in the long grass

like thousands and thousands
of perched birds watching,

closing his eyes
and breathing

in the gentle breeze
slowly circling and gathering

in little eddies at his neck,
which he was not,

because he could be killed
for anything, anything,

but he did look quickly behind him
into this rotten house,

the beams sagging with must,
the plaster dropping in sticky flakes of flesh,

before twisting his name,
Frank Jennings,

into a wick
he lit

and tossed burning inside the house
while pulling his other leg through,

gathering up what had just been cargo,
what had just been loot,

thrown overboard
for the insurance

(Breathe.)
(Breathe.)

his body
his life

gathering himself up
in his thin arms,

turning toward the unknown,
and stealing away,

and in the photograph
I found and am holding

in my hands
the grandmother

leans against the doorjamb
made of thick timbers

with an undulating grain, pierced
periodically with knots,

like the tear-stained
eyes of elephants,

like terraced fields or
wakes ululating behind a vessel,

her chin is up and jaw tilted just so
as though chewing, or maybe

running her tongue where a molar used to be,
or contemplating a taste in her mouth,

or preparing to spit,
or looking for a clod

of clay or better yet a fist
sized rock to smash in a thousand shards

the looking
this camera wants to do

to her boy
capture him

for she knows
for the insurance,

for she knows what they could do
more than anyone,

she knows what they do
more than anyone,

and her muscled forearms are fortressed
across the diagonal striped pattern

of her dress which toward the knee has two holes,
and suddenly like that her dress becomes

a map of the trades,
the holes the bodies

of islands cast in the windcombed sea,
and beneath the dress

a short sleeved lace shirt,
the collar of which elegantly droops

atop the diagonals,
and you will notice as well

on a loop of string circling her neck
a key somehow not where gravity would pull it

but poised almost perfectly
opposite her heart,

and just behind her,
from the darkness

a child
peeking out

looking out into the distance,
which might be the distant eye

of this camera,
which happens also to be,

now,
this poem,

and though she doesn't
touch the boy,

the boy is hers
my own white mother

how many times told
by white people

that brown child is not yours,
that curly-headed sun-loved thing

you nursed and whose ass
you wiped the shit from

and whose very body you bore
of your florid gore

(at which, for the record, my mother here
would say, *That's a little much, Rossy*),

the many knives in her body,
in her mouth,

my mother did not know were there,
sharpening, until in the supermarket,

standing in the checkout,
some woman, some white

woman, staring at my white mom,
alabaster in a daisy-speckled sundress,

in Painesville, Ohio,
my brother riding shotgun in the cart,

me on her hip,
head tucked into her shoulder,

away from the looking,
probably making almost a face

of disbelief, as she turned round
and round in her mind

the impossibility
of this maternal scene,

no calculus to accommodate
what she's looking at,

her brow furrowed in stupefaction
as she cranks us round and round

in the petite aperture
of her white

imagination,
and my mother by now

rocking the cart back and forth
a little faster, my brother dozing

from the rocking, all the while
holding me on her hip,

and seeing
the not seeing,

Mom opened her blade
untenderly to the gawker

trying to fix us
by looking up from her *TV Guide*

and, in a voice
approaching the Luciferian,

counseled,
Yes they're mine

and I have the stretch marks to prove it,
and cut like that the eyes

from the woman's head,
her reflection

disappearing for now
with the blade

my mother methodically folded
and planted into her pocket

with the other daisies
grinning on her sundress,

my mother and her knives
make a garden,

one of the many linguistic varieties
of the more familiar

what are you
what the fuck are you

looking at
which utterance

can also be discharged
as a look

in the Arkansas sun,
for you're the one bought the aviator hat

the child wears,
pulled snug,

the long flap on the right side
framing the tender line

of his jaw,
the face somehow of a dreamer

which you in this photo
do not seem to be,

though put the dream
of flight

on the child's head,
which he leans shy into the doorjamb

for he too knows
he's being looked at,

he knows
he's being shot,

he's being shared,
by someone who doesn't love him,

and so does not give his whole body
to the camera,

and I notice, I see,
the soft cast of that child's gaze,

which, if we zoom into his peach leaf eye,
we see that he's not quite looking

at the camera looking
at him, but rather, somehow, beyond it,

his aviator hat's goggles
catching the light

which comes from the dream
inside the boy's head

of flight
his grandmother made

despite,
and looking closer

at the boy's
looking you notice,

following the clean denim jacket
and white collared shirt beneath it,

which emerges at his forearms
in crisply rolled cuffs,

in his right hand
he shelters something almost

floral, a rose perhaps,
pale yellow, or even, you think,

maybe he holds the nave
of a magnolia bloom,

or it could be, it's true,
a few bills, a little money,

but by enlarging the boy
until he fills the field of my vision

I can see
it's an origami bird

he has made,
and on which he might,

with his left hand,
be putting the finishing touches

to the beak,
that the bird might better lullaby,

the wings folded lightly
against his fingers,

the bird's sharp head twisted back
toward the child,

looking into his dream
of the sky,

but the bird, also,
cranes her little paper neck

back in the direction
of the grandmother,

who, the more I study her,
despite what I said before,

moving her eyes as close to me
as they will come,

moving mine as close to her
as they will go,

seems to be,
it is true,

looking into the sky beyond,
looking into

the sky beyond
the photographer taking the picture,

taking her boy,
and bringing the child

as close to us as possible,
the little galaxies of light lustering

his beautiful brown skin,
his lower lip and nose,

if we bring him so close to us
we can hear him breathing,

the soft eddying of wind into his nose,
and closer still,

until his lungs become kites,
let's make them today

of newspaper dyed purple and
flesh with peonies

and pokeberries
and the black walnut husks

soothing in rainwater out back,
let's make them

today with gold
smudges of dandelion

lighting the diamond of newsprint
framed with four sinewy sticks of dogwood,

so that, as the kites fledge
into the sky

above the sunflower field
in the boy's body,

they look like
hands greeting us,

they look like all the beloving
hands who have ferried that child forth,

beckoning us into the precious sky
inside the child,

skipping into the gusts,
pirouetting and tugging

the strings in our hands
which we wind around our wrists

to keep the kites,
the child,

all the beloving
that is the child,

from flying away,
as the sky in the boy

slowly blackens and swells
luminous with stars,

the kites now invisible
except for their clapping or laughing

in the night wind, or when
flickering in the web

of starlight inside the boy,
tugging taut the tether in our hands,

which is the sound
of the child

we can hear
breathing

so close
so close

our bodies now
a kind of shield

our looking now
a kind of shield

between the boy
and the looking

between myself
and the looking

I too find myself doing
now holding

my breath
how do we be

holding the child
so broken are we

by the breaking
and the looking

how do we be
holding each other

so broken are we by
the breaking and the looking

so ill am I
how do we

cut it out,
the eyes from our heads,

inside the goggle
on the boy's head

a star of light
is splayed like a body

in flight,
or the body is splayed

like a star
inside the body of the boy,

we're the ones put the hat on him
at 4:56 a.m.,

the Doctor gasping finally through
the ghosts of light,

legs splayed into a star,
and when he emerges,

the right hand swoops so low,
a pelican or cormorant

merging with her reflection
in the water,

before pulling the ball slowly,
so slowly, toward the rim,

which involves every single muscle
in his flying body

quivered into a singular
coherence, the way

we bring a child's head
to our hip to say

you're ok,
I'm here,

Kareem and Jamaal and Landsberger
and the whole Spectrum

silent except for the cooing mouths
of their hands extended

toward Doc, toward
each other,

this flight
makes us be,

and Doc holding the pill
like a skull, gently,

not Hamlet in the least,
but the way we do

with the knowing
our bodies have unknowingly,

call it tenderness,
he is *tending*,

reaching so far
like this, he could be

planting seeds, he seems to be,
he is, crawling,

when he releases
the ball,

at last, with the wrist-twist
that makes the orb kiss

the glass with what
we used to call *English*,

but tonight forward,
for the turning toward

Doc makes the ball do,
Doc in flight makes the ball do,

Doc in flight decides
to make the ball do,

kissing, let's call it *kissing,*
this endless reaching

we do
—breathe—

crawling as reaching
like this sometimes makes us

be, splayed like a star,
sprawling, though

Erving's crawling
is through the air,

and as such has the quality
of both soaring and swimming,

though, if we look closely,
Doc has reached

already his flight's apex,
and the crawling the reaching is

is a way
of not falling,

the reaching is a way
of not falling,

and you're goddamned right
I'm going to bring my father

into this poem,
that's just how it goes

with me,
crawling into it,

as he is
not most prominently

in my memory, in my body,
though occasionally, for instance

crawling in reaching
in flight

from his bed to the bathroom
where the meds for his

diverticulitis sat on the counter,
in a pain from the strawberries

he couldn't resist,
a cluster of sweetness

beckoning then wrecking him
(please don't blame the strawberries,

never blame the strawberries),
but he had to get to work,

something stupid that he hated
to be clear,

(though truth be told
it was a treat,

the occasional family dinners
at Burger King

when he'd load us up,
chicken sandwich no mayo for me,

whopper with cheese for my brother,
always the largest fries possible,

mom something dietish oh
and sodas! sodas!

smuggling himself
from behind the counter

to sit a few minutes with us
at our plastic booth

giddy in our cholesterol
and ketchup)

and so he was crawling toward
the amber cylinder of relief,

less poetically known as
amoxicillin,

and lord it is not devotion
to work I am lauding,

god forbid,
nor the shitstorm of the nuclear family,

I am simply
looking at the reaching

crawling sometimes is,
in this instance

my father
toward who he loved,

which is a kind of flying
my Dad does sometimes

in my body,
the trillion tiny splayed stars

my body is made of my father
reaching to keep from falling,

do you know the mangrove
do you know the mycelial ballet

who were human
long long before we were

and remained so
long long after,

reaching to keep
from falling,

and lonely for him
I sometimes will study

my own hands,
which are his hands,

recalling the way he held
my brother's and my heads

through the crosswalk,
or how he would hold

like a glass of prosecco
one of the lilies my mother planted,

lowering his face
to the flute

and breathing,
and breathing,

and closing his eyes,
and resting,

how badly I want
my father to be resting,

and resting,
and smiling,

in the breathing,
and the breathing,

and surface with his nose
kissed with the gold

kissing lilies do,
or more ambitious

I look into the true impossibility
of this body this cargo

this loot this star
magnolia bloom just shoved itself

from the velvet nipple
of its bud,

its womb,
offering its fragrance

into the world,
the small grove

inside my body
which is my father

waving his flowers at me,
reaching toward me

to keep me from falling,
as he would

down the shore,
the crummy boardwalk

at Seaside Heights blathering,
the waft of fried

everything, and carnival jangles
beyond, and my dad,

younger than me now,
not far from where he'd been

briefly stationed when he dodged
being drafted—

murdering and being
murdered,

which is called
elsewhere *war*,

called elsewhere *intervention*,
not what it is,

thrown overboard
for the insurance—

by enlisting in the navy
the very day his number was called

(which sage counsel came from his Dad,
my Poppa, among the beloving),

joining a meteorology team
called the 100-knotters

for the number of typhoons
over the Philippine Sea

into the eyes of which
they flew,

which flight aided
and abetted the murder,

and flying like this
tried sadly

to prove himself
a citizen,

not cargo loot
thrown overboard

for the insurance
for anything they can,

I glimpse my mother
beneath the umbrella

on the towel with our flip-flops and t-shirts,
her elbow on the red and white Igloo

stocked with hard salami sandwiches
and Juicy Juice and plums,

watching not smiling,
her right hand making and unmaking

fists in the sand,
around his neck

we'd wrap our arms,
my brother and me,

and become
in the surf rising

to meet us
like scrawny brown wings

on our dad's back
gusting in the tumult

he would drag
through until

the hands of the water
held us up,

and he said
big breath,

and clinging
to his slick manatee

shoulders we plunged
airborne, the invisible

chrysalis cloaking our little
bodies bursting

as he reached
through the water,

pulling us with him,
reaching toward him

to keep from sailing off,
how many million eyes in the wake

flashing their light at us
clinging to one another,

lit by their looking,
and how my face to my

dad's shoulder,
my shoulder

to my brother's face,
was a kind of breathing,

and soaring,
as a child

I could breathe underwater,
my father pulling us

through the thick air,
pulling us through

the pulling us
by reaching

his arms as far forward as he could
and dragging them back

toward us to keep us
from falling,

to keep from falling,
like that he'd be holding us,

and in this way
flew some from the overboard,

and likewise showed us
how to fly some from the overboard,

by reaching toward
what you love,

which is not a citizenship
we talking about,

but a practice,
despite the hold,

a practice that spites the hold,
spites the overboard,

we in here talking
about the reaching

that makes of falling flight,
do you see

what I'm saying,
we're in here talking

about holding each other,
which is a practice, we

talking about holding
our breath,

how long have we been,
and how can I be

holding yours,
and you

be holding mine,
this is my question,

I think,
how might I be

holding your breathing
and you be

holding mine,
a practice

we talking about,
the reaching that makes

of falling flight,
we in here

talking about
the practice

of the beholden,
a practice

of being beholden,
talking about

how might I hold
my beholden out to you

and you hold yours out to me,
how do we be holding each other,

how do we be
beholden to each other,

which is really to say,
how do we be,

a practice
we talking about,

a practice, might be, that we, in here,
talking about joy,

we in here
talking about joy,

which might be to say,
depending on how you look at it,

we in here talking about destroying the world
for the world,

bound in gratitude
like this

in the beholden,
beholding like this

the beholden,
what then,

in the photo
I am beholden now

the two women
run toward the camera,

the one in tank top and shorts,
arms and legs lit by the flash,

by the light coming through the small window
atop the camera,

coming through the window
of my office now,

limning into stars the forsythia
just opening her golden eyes,

tensed as though
in movement

because she is running
toward the camera,

she is being moved
by the looking

toward the looking,
her right hand nearly

a fist and shouting
at the looking,

at the person behind the camera,
there are flowers growing

on her shirt,
vining from her hip

nearly to her clavicle,
it is wisteria

and clematis,
a swirl of pollinating creatures,

including you and me,
carouse and amble and hover

in her wake,
we gather

in the wake of the garden
this looking makes,

the muscles in her neck
cast shadows, for she is really

shouting, and running,
toward the window

and the light laughing in
like she is going to

bound through it,
she is going to fly through it,

as the woman to her left
moves also quickly and with determination

toward the looking,
her scarf casting left

in the breeze
her hustling makes,

and there is something
about her gaze

through the camera
that reminds me in my body

is a tree slouched in prayer
by its burden of butterflies,

reminds me
I am one of the butterflies,

that inside me always is a lifting off
in the direction of something else,

toward *you*, I really mean to say,
waiting to happen,

which is among the ways of saying
this looking makes me breathe,

this looking holds
my breathing,

it does not capture or shoot anyone,
does not fix anyone,

does not catalog or corral
or specimen or coerce,

but holds them both
in their flight,

moving as they are,
moved as they are,

away from nothing,
but rather toward

this holding,
this beholden,

looking as though
descending a great staircase made of air with joy,

a good title for this photo,
as though running down a great staircase made of air with joy,

for running too is a kind
of falling

again and again,
as running toward what you love

and what loves you
is a kind of falling

again and again
into the reaching

that makes of falling flight,
into the hold

of the beholden we are,
just as Doc does

after all that flying,
he falls,

as the ball kisses the window
and drops through the net,

he falls,
painlessly and temporarily,

crawling for a few seconds
before getting to his feet,

and we,
watching,

reaching toward
each other,

we breathe

Acknowledgments

Nothing I write I write by myself. Everything I write, by which I mean everything, I write with and for and from others, which is a way of saying, always, *debt*. Which is a way of saying, always, *gratitude*. A way of saying, always, *I am beholden*. The older I get the more beautiful this becomes to me—how much, how completely, I am made by others. How I can sometimes trace an overt lineage in my work, but how more often than not, I know this to be true (how could it not?), the lineage disappears into me. Or it shows up later, giving a reading, and thinking, mid-poem, Oh, Gerald Stern gave me this line (this happens to me often), thank you, Gerry! Or: oh, June Jordan, hello! Thank you, June Jordan! There goes Toi, there goes Yusef, there goes Marie. Oh, Neruda! Hello! Thank you! Thank you, Patrick. Thank you, Ara. Thank you, Ruth Ellen (Szzy!). Thank you, Steve. Etc. Etc. Etc. Etc. Etc. You know what I mean. Perhaps this is one of the evidences of being truly moved—"you" are not only moved but "you" are also moved into. "You" are disappeared into. Your breath is so much more than your breath. Your body so many bodies. Your poems given to you. The cities inside us, all of whom spoke us, thought us, dreamt us, dream us into being.

This joy-ning is not without a little ambivalence sometimes in the world-destroying horseshit capitalist nightmare fantasy of the individual. Oh shit, I've never made anything by myself! Oh shit, I maybe am not a myself! Oh shit, I *definitely* am not a myself!

Oh shit, it's all been given to me. It's all been given to me. Oh. O. Thank you.

A poem's practice, the practice of poetry, must always defy the logics of property. By which I mean practicing the truth of gift and gratitude. Robin Wall Kimmerer, thank you! My breath is made possible by the breath of others. My breath is the breath of others. My is not my, and how could it ever be? And who would want it so? *We talking about practice. We owe each other everything.*

I want to honor the mycelial way poems are made, but not only poems. Lives. Our lives, each other's lives, I'm saying. The black walnut tree dappling the morning sun coming through the window. The blue jay alighted in the shadows long enough to sing something that entered this singing. All that which has moved into me so deeply that I don't even know it wasn't always there. All the singing that makes this singing. All the singing without which this little song would not be. All the singing. All the beloving. All the generations. Who loved you before they knew you. More than we will ever know. Gratitude.

*

I was deep in a few books as I was completing this poem, and one of them is Christina Sharpe's *In The Wake: On Blackness and Being*. I read Sharpe's book (recommended by my friend Nzingha, thank you!) in a stretch of time during which I thought I might never "finish" this poem, a poem which at that time was still called *Flight* (one of the subtitles, by the way, in my mind, and now in yours). Which is to say, Sharpe's book reminded me before the fact that this book was called, at least one of the titles anyway, *Be Holding*.

Had "I" not read *In the Wake* "I" doubt "I" would have finished this poem. Maybe "I" would've finished another poem, but "I" wouldn't have finished this one. *The wake, aspiration, beholden-ness*: these all come, in *Be Holding*, from *In the Wake*. Sharpe's work showed this poem, finally, how to breathe. How to behold, and how to behold itself. It is a "map to be held."

Sharpe writes, "In what ways might we enact a beholden-ness to each other, laterally?," and "How are we beholden to and beholders of each other in ways that change across time and place and space and yet remain? Beholden in the wake, as, at the very least, if we are lucky, an opportunity (back to the door) in our black bodies to try to look, try to see."

Endless gratitude and indebtedness to *In the Wake* for understanding this poem before I did. And I hope this poem to be a kind of thinking with, as well as a thinking from, and a *thinking after—* after as in time, and after as in influence or inspiration or aspiration or breath, as in: *Be Holding*, after Christina Sharpe's *In the Wake*. But also after as in care. Like *looking after*.

And Aracelis Girmay's whole body of work—of course, of course— but particularly her book *The Black Maria*, to which *Be Holding* is also bound in gratitude. Working on this poem in Umbertide, where you brought me: reading *The Black Maria* in a garden, beside a castle, beside the sorrows, beside the centuries, and the laughter. I am indebted to so much language and thought and feeling and care from your books/hearts, I mean, I don't know how to write poems without them (I don't know how to *be* without them), but

Be Holding is especially talking to and with and from and for the poem "The Black Maria":

> This poem
>
> wants only the moon in its hair and the boy on the roof.
>
> This boy on the roof of this poem
>
> with a moon in his heart. . . .
>
> . . .
>
> splayed & sighing as a star in my arms.
>
> Maybe he will be the boy who studies stars.

Which is to say, too: *Be Holding*, after Aracelis Girmay. Gratitude.

And Patrick Rosal, whose poem "Boys' Bodies in Flight (are also a kind of text)," rings throughout this poem (I should say—is among the gathering of Rosal poems always in mine; a murmuration of them; every poem "I" write feels truly like a collaboration with you, if not a theft; there goes Trees again; there goes the birds; truly, I wonder if I'd even write poems without you, family), especially these lines:

> Doesn't everyone
>
> know of boys who dream
> repeatedly of wings
>
> And yet
>
> so few of us know what to tell them

Be Holding, after Patrick Rosal. Gratitude.

Amiri Baraka's "An Agony. As Now." comes through: "slits in the metal for eyes." This is the poem that made me start reading and writing poems. ("I am inside someone / who hates me. I look / out from his eyes.") But also this sentence of his, which I can't find in a book, though it has lived in my body, has been shaping this poem, since I first heard him say it some decades ago: "At the bottom of the Atlantic Ocean there's a railroad made of human bones." And finally (you know by now there is no finally to this), this sentence I transcribed from a reading I watched online, a sentence I also cannot find in a book, so do not know exactly how to attribute it (though you can look it up), except as a guiding and girding understanding of this poem, and a guiding understanding period: "The preparation for pain is minimal. For joy, a lifetime." After Baraka.

And while we're talking about debt, the debt I'm speaking of, the "bad debt" I'm speaking of, is informed by the chapter "Debt and Study" in *The Undercommons*, which is among the most important things I've ever read and is deep in the thinking this book is trying to do. *Be Holding* is trying to practice a practice, an indebtedness, a way, a holding, that is indebted, in-(bad)-debted to Stefano Harney and Fred Moten. A practice of the beholden. Which is also called gratitude. Is also called joy. *We owe each other everything.* After that.

Likewise Saidiya Hartman's *Wayward Lives, Beautiful Experiments.* And M. NourbeSe Philip's *Zong!* Of course. Of course. And Kris Manjapra's essay "Plantation Dispossessions." And Garnette Cadogan, who says "walking is falling again and again." And Toi Derricotte, whose practice of looking, and looking inside, and looking at the looking, and the reaching that might come of that, has been one of the truest guides I know. And Kevin Quashie, for *The Sovereignty of Quiet*, who reminds us of the brea(d)th of our expression. Reminds us, too, that it is *aliveness* we're talking about. Aliveness. Gratitude. And Hanif Abdurraqib, who planted a few more flowers in this poem. And Kamasi Washington's song "Askim," which helped me with the shape of this poem. And that line from Fred Moten's poem "hard enough to enjoy" in *The Little Edges*: "Dancing is what / we make of falling," which has been a breath inside the writing of this poem. And, of course, Allen Iverson. A. I. Elephant heart. The crossover, yes, but to play *with such love*. That's the practice we in here talking about. That's the looking inside this looking. Gratitude. And Faith Ringgold's *Tar Beach*. And Zoe Strauss's *South Philly (Mattress Flip Front)*. And Charles Burnett. And Kevin Everson. And Carrie Mae Weems. Bound in gratitude. And Grover Washington Jr.'s "Let It Flow (for Dr. J)." And the last ten or fifteen minutes of Richard Pryor's *Live on the Sunset Strip*. And Don Belton, who, the more I think of it, truly taught me the questions of this poem. Asked me again and again: *What are you looking at?* Again and again, he asked me: *What are you studying? What are you practicing?* All the breathing that makes this breath. All the voices that are this voice.

And Toni Morrison's *Playing in the Dark* and *Beloved*, bell hooks's *Black Looks*, and Susan Sontag's *On Photography* and *Regarding the Pain of Others*. And a conversation in a kitchen in Pittsburgh after a panel in a library that ended with laughter. There is an image of us reaching toward each other in laughter. Holding each other in laughter. And something I heard Tim Seibles say once I think that I'll never forget, that also is the breath, the breathing, in this poem. You too put the breath in this poem. And J. Kameron Carter, for letting me sit in on his class where he made me know, oh right, what I really mean is:

we talking about destroying the world

for *the earth*

We talking about *the earth*. And he's talking about Ed Roberson. And I'm talking about Soul Fire Farm, and the 2015 BIPOC farmer training program, where I was reminded that the beholding, the being held, the beholden, is a practice and a study that begins with the land. The *earth*. Where I thought, in that first gathering circle in 2015, *oh, this is beholding. This is regard. This is gratitude. This is the practice*. Bound in it.

It is endless, this.

And Anni and Wendy Lee for that independent study we did, the little cracks those conversations made. And all the students from that workshop—that work*out*—in fall of 2018. That lab of care and wonder that we practiced at making. That we keep practicing at making. Janan, Austin, Brianna, Soleil, Noah, Lauren, Meredith, Anni, Gionni, Susan, Alberto, Rose. And Big Baby Noey, for playing ball and talking about trees (a good subtitle for this book, by the way: *playing ball and talking about trees*). And everyone I've ever played ball with—unless they called too many fouls. A little digression here to say, gratitude to the lab of care and wonder pickup (i.e., real) basketball is, the practice in a kind of social life, working it out, negotiating the terms of our being together play by play, game by game, court by court. Kin-making. The best ref always no ref. You heard that? *The best ref no ref.* (Not only because I'm a hack.) The ones I lived at (Vets, Delaware, Seger Park), and the ones I've been a guest at. I've learned to be a guest at. Gratitude.

And everyone I've ever talked about trees with. Or thought about trees with. Or looked into trees with. Or planted trees with. Or loved trees with. And every tree that's ever held me or listened to me or cared for me or fed me or cooled me, or would. Every tree I mean. Bound in gratitude.

And to all the beloveds who have listened to or read versions of this poem, or parts of this poem, or asked questions or made points or corrections (Landsberger a *decent* athlete, Kareem the *best player of all time*, etc.) or head-fakes or tossed a dumb line into the bleachers or said *what about this* or *you know what* or *remember when*, which is to say, all the beloving, among them (sorry to whom I forget, this list is longer and longer than this): Kayte, Alex, Jon, Young David, Yalie, Bgbg, Adrian, Lotl, Gabby, Walton, Wally, Hammy, Boogie, Skeety, Biggie Mommy, Gerry, Johnny Mums, Ama, Terri, Abdel, Sam, Mykey, Vaughany, and dear Chrism, who in the very beginning of this poem told me to keep going. To stay in it. Steve, for the loving looking, for the wonder. And of course Poppa, whose knowledge of Lakers history, all NBA history actually, is prodigious, voluminous, and who, in more ways than I can say, has held this poem. And Scot-y with the Bod-y, who never tired of replaying the flying, who never tires of the flying, walking on the earth the way Doc walks in the sky—thank you for asking for this poem. Giving a real shit, I mean. This poem is for you. Essence, for looking and looking and wondering with me through this poem. Seeing things I could not. The study. Thank you. And, always, dear Steffieboo, to whom I first read part of this poem under a peach tree in blossom, with bees, and a blanket. Who kept wondering, like me, how is he going to make this shot? Encouragement and care and listening and sharing. Love and gratitude. So much.

And Kareem Abdul-Jabbar. Thank you.

And, of course, Julius Erving. Dr. J. The Doctor. The Flight. The Practice. The Study. Thank you.

To Ed Ochester, Maria Sticco, Joel W. Coggins, Alex Wolfe, and everyone at University of Pittsburgh Press for their patience and kindness and care: thank you.

To the places and institutions that have supported me in various ways while I've been working on this poem: the Guggenheim Foundation, ICCI, The Radcliffe Institute (and The Rainbow!), Civitella Ranieri, the Vermont Studio Center, and Indiana University, for the beloved, brilliant students I get to study with, practice with. And always Cave Canem, for the work you have done and will do; for letting me practice some of this poem for the first time in 2015.

And to my mother and brother. How lucky I am for you. How much gratitude.

And my father. The Reaching. The Holding. The Caring. The Flying.

And especially to my Nana and Poppa and Uncle Roy and Aunt Butter and Uncle Ernest and Uncle Bennett and Aunt Truly and Aunt Verna and Uncle Sid and so so so many more for all the holding. All the beholding. All the beloving. And my great-grandmother Biggie, who I did not know but who knew me. Who put the hat on us.

And reader, always, always: thank you.

This never ends.

Bound in gratitude

Image Credits

Fig 1. (p. 9) Julius Erving #6 of the Philadelphia 76ers drives to the basket in what becomes known as "The Move" against Mark Landsberger #54 and Kareem Abdul-Jabbar #33 of the Los Angeles Lakers during game 4 of the NBA Finals on May 11 at the Spectrum in Philadelphia, Pennsylvania. Photo by Manny Millan / Sports Illustrated via Getty Images

Figs 2 & 3. (pp. 25–26) *Hands on Sycamore*, photographs by Stephanie Smith.

Fig 4. (p. 43) Julius Erving #6 of the Philadelphia 76ers drives to the basket in what becomes known as "The Move" against Mark Landsberger #54 and Kareem Abdul-Jabbar #33 of the Los Angeles Lakers during game 4 of the NBA Finals on May 11 at the Spectrum in Philadelphia, Pennsylvania. Photo by Jim Cummins / NBAE / Getty Images.

Fig 5. (p. 60) "This Negro woman lives with her husband and two grandchildren in an old converted schoolhouse. All the rest of her children have left the county. Heard County, Georgia," photo by Jack Delano. Library of Congress Prints and Photographs Division Washington, D.C. 20540 USA.

Fig 6. (p. 93) *Welcome Home*, photography by and copyright Carrie Mae Weems. Courtesy of the artist and Jack Shainman Gallery, New York.